CW00550134

In loving memory of
Elsie Honeywell
1923-2022

Elsie Honeywell's Wartime Diary

PREFACE

Elsie Honeywell, my mother, was born in 1923 in Clitheroe, Lancashire. She was at the same time a very ordinary, and most extraordinary, person. She had only just left school when the Second World War broke out, and like many people of her generation was called on to do astonishing things at a very young age, in her case in the Civil Nursing Reserve.

In later life she was full of tales about 'the old days', and eventually we persuaded her (it wasn't difficult!) to write as much down as she wanted, and so this diary was born. It wasn't over-long, but we think it was a *tour de force* and very worthy of publication. She would have approved.

Aged 98 she finally realised that living at home was getting too difficult and came to live with me and my wife Valerie for her last few months. Even then she was reasonably fit for her age and 100% competent mentally – or as we say in Lancashire, *"She had all her chairs at home"*.

But old age takes its toll on everyone, and three days after her 99th birthday she quietly drifted away with family at her bedside.

She would have loved the idea of you now enjoying her brief diary. She actually wrote it around 2015, and I have taken the liberty of adding a few chapters, particularly with reference to the later years and her children. There are also some references in Mum's diary to places which have changed significantly, so if you see any text in [square brackets] that indicates a bit of my description.

Elsie Honeywell's Wartime Diary

Chapter One

In July 1939 I left Clitheroe Royal Grammar School aged 15. [At that time the Grammar School existed only on York Street – the newer building on Chatburn Road wasn't built until the 1950s, when it was the Girls' Grammar School, the boys remaining at York Street.]

The Grammar School on York Street, Clitheroe, now the CRGS 6th form centre.

Due to yet another bout of tonsillitis I missed the end of my school years but had recovered sufficiently by the 8th of August to begin work at Clitheroe Shirtings Ltd in Grindleton as a stock clerk [The old Clitheroe Shirtings building was near the river – it was demolished several years ago and replaced by The Spinney and a large office building.]

Three evenings a week were spent at the Technical School for shorthand, bookkeeping, and maths. These classes were held in the Grammar School building on York Street, so the classrooms were familiar.

My friend Doreen Houlker and I had known each other as far back as I can remember. The same midwife had delivered Doreen at home two days before she delivered me at no. 4 Bonny Grass Terrace [Woone Lane]. We had attended Council School aged five, Pendle Junior School when it was newly built in 1932, the Grammar School aged 11, and started work together in 1939.

In church on Sunday September 3rd, at the end of the service, we learned that war had been declared. I vaguely remember an air-raid siren wailing – just testing, we were told. It wasn't long before many of our contemporaries were leaving Clitheroe for the Army, Navy, and Air Force. The town became a training centre and khaki uniforms were everywhere.

The Royal Artillery came first, in the old Carlton Mill [now the site of Howdens and Hargreaves Plumbers], then No. 1 TBRE Royal Engineers took over Low Moor Mill [a huge former cotton mill, owned by the Garnett family since 1799 which closed in 1930].

A YMCA was set up in Moor Lane Sunday School. Volunteers served tea and coffee, Spam, cheese, and jam sandwiches, and many of the boys were invited into people's homes.

Saturday nights in the ballroom at the Conservative Club [on Castle Street] were very popular with the local girls, as were 'tanner hops' in the Parish Church School mid-week.

We went to first-aid classes and to fire-watching lectures and were shown how to operate stirrup pumps.

Food was rationed and many people grew their own vegetables in gardens and allotments. Vegetable peelings and food scraps were saved in a bucket for friends who kept a pig, and we looked forward to some black market pork when the pig was killed.

There were wartime activities for men not needed in the forces – as air-raid wardens, the Home Guard and in the fire service.

Many families had taken evacuees from Manchester and other cities. Dorothy Bond, a cousin from Hull, often came to spend the weekend, and catch up on sleep having spent many nights during the week in an air-raid shelter. I looked forward to her visits.

Dorothy was a buyer for the fabric department in a well-known department store in Hull and usually brought some 'redundant samples'! Her gifts helped a great deal with the shortage of clothing coupons. Her nephew Colin also stayed with us during a heavy period of air raids on Hull, and he went to Pendle Junior School.

After some time teenagers and girls in their twenties had to register either for the forces, or to work on munitions or other important occupations. One by one, girls left Clitheroe Shirtings Ltd, and older married girls took their place.

Doreen and I considered our options and wrote for details of the Civil Nursing Reserve. In reply we each received an identical letter requesting us to attend Calderstones Hospital at Whalley for a medical exam – so much for information!

Chapter 2

Meanwhile, life went on.

One warm, sunny Monday evening in July 1942, and after listening to a fire-watching lecture, our route home took us through the castle grounds. We saw three members of the Royal Engineers eating fish and chips. They were forbidden to be seen eating in the streets, so had found a hidden corner in one of the shelters near the bandstand. Boys being boys, they didn't fail to notice us and offered to share their chips with us!

The bandstand in the grounds of Clitheroe Castle – which still exists!

Roy's Auntie Annette said later it was 'fate' that we came along just then. Two days later we went to the 'tanner hop' and met two of the boys again; one was called Freddie. We arranged to meet again on Saturday at the Conservative Club, and Freddie walked me home.

As their unit, 66 War Party, was leaving on Monday to go to Chatham, we met again on Sunday evening and the following day several of us went to Clitheroe station to say goodbye. Quite a few local girls were sorry to see them go, but this was wartime and similar goodbyes happened all the time.

It wasn't unusual to just get to know someone, and then they were gone. On Thursday, however, a letter arrived. The postmark was Chatham and that was the first of many from Freddie. By the beginning of August several letters had been exchanged.

Because 66 War Party had not had their normal privilege leave when they were at Low Moor, they were now able to take seven days leave from Chatham. Fred expressed a wish to return to Clitheroe, as did Sadie, his friend, and no doubt one or two more.

Initially it was suggested that they would stay back at Low Moor, but Pop (my father) after thinking very hard, invited Fred to spend his leave at no. 32 [Salthill Road, the family home], and with Sadie and his girlfriend Renée Wrigley we enjoyed their leave together. Later we were to learn that Sadie had lost a leg in France shortly after D-Day.

Freddie's next leave was in November, and I was invited to Buckfastleigh in Devon to meet his family. Fred's mother Amy wore a caliper after a hip operation had left one leg shorter than the other (there were no artificial hip replacements in 1942.)

Jack, Fred's father, worked for the Co-op at that time, and was responsible for collecting fresh fish from Plymouth.

He had also worked as a mechanic in Kingsbridge servicing Western National buses. Amy was the eldest of four girls, whilst Jack was the youngest of four boys.

Fred was the eldest of three brothers. Bill, 13 months younger, was soon to join the Royal Artillery. Arthur, another two years younger, was in training with the Observer Corps to identify aircraft. He later went overseas with the US Navy on D-Day and said his biggest worry was preventing the US forces from shooting down every plane, for not all were the enemy!

Roy & Elsie saunter along Paignton seafront, 1942.

Meeting the family I was to learn that Frederick Roy's name at home was Roy, so he was Roy to me from then on.

There was a lot of Devon for me to discover. We travelled by bus to Plymouth and saw for ourselves the results of the heavy bombing they had experienced. We visited Amy's sisters, Manda with her husband Tom and Bessie, with husband Harold, in Buckfastleigh, and Edith in Newton Abbot.

There we sampled Edith's home-made elderberry wine. Jack's brother Frank lived in Paignton with his wife Annette. They owned a jewellery shop. I remember there being a heavy cabinet-type air-raid shelter in one room of their house.

We walked on the sea front at Paignton and were photographed by a man who gave us his card. We later collected the photograph which is now on our mantelpiece.

We also visited the two Grans and one Granfer several times and took the family dog, Kim, for walks on Wallaford Down.

Chapter 3

In January Roy had another week's leave and came back to Clitheroe. It was during that week that Doreen and I went to Calderstones EMS [Emergency Medical Service] Hospital for a so-called medical. It was only a matter of days later that we had another letter telling us to report to Whittingham EMS Hospital near Preston.

Whittingham Hospital probably in the 1950s. Raphael Tuck & Sons Ltd.

This was part of a large complex of old red brick buildings which formed a fairly self-contained mental hospital. There was a church, a laundry, a farm, a bakery, an X-ray department, and dispensary all within the grounds, and several blocks containing wards for the mentally ill. One of these blocks was taken over by the EMS.

On February 23rd 1943 Doreen and I, along with ten other girls, arrived at the hospital. There we were issued with our uniforms: three blue-striped dresses, six white aprons and three white caps. We were allocated rooms in one of the blocks in the grounds of the mental hospital.

It was bitterly cold; two iron beds and harsh grey blankets – a somewhat grim introduction of what was to come. We discovered that we could fill hot water bottles downstairs in the large kitchen, and it wasn't long before we realized that it was unwise to switch on the light and walk straight in. The trick was to reach for the light switch, turn it on and close the door, then after a few seconds, walk in. This way it gave the cockroaches chance to scuttle out of sight!

I was told to report to Sister Anderson on Ward 55, a surgical ward, and was given two St John Ambulance handbooks, 'Home Nursing' and 'First Aid'. These were the first and last of our training manuals! I was initiated into the secrets of 'hospital corners' [a way of folding sheets when making a bed] by a nurse from Clitheroe. I learnt how to sweep and polish the wooden floors, clean the sluice room, clean the lockers, and serve the meals.

Part of the afternoons were spent in a side ward, studying the little St John's books.

After two weeks we were called to matron's office, one by one. She was one of the old school of matrons, very severe-looking and Irish. We expected a kind of exam on what we had learnt so far. We need not have worried. She asked me "Well nurse, do you think you can stand it after all!

I signed an official card on March 8th and then I was a member of the Civil Nursing Reserve. I was told to go to Ward 60, an ENT Ward, and report to Sister Whitehead.

Apart from Sister, I think every other nurse on Ward 60 had either a husband or boyfriend in the forces. When Sister returned from Matron's office each morning, we were all pleased if she brought some letters for us.

We started duty on the Ward at 7 am. First breakfast was at 7:30 and second breakfast at 8:20; a long time to go without even a cup of tea. We had three hours off during the day and handed over to night staff at 8 pm.

My pay packet contained all of £1 1s 4d! [£1.06!] Sister White, the Home sister, sat at the end of the long table in the dining room when we received our pay packet, and we were expected to buy Government Savings Stamps from her. When we had collected 15s-worth [£0.75p] we could exchange them for a savings certificate.

With the bus fare home once a week, one evening to Preston to see a film, postage stamps etc., the money didn't go very far.

Chapter 4

I looked forward to receiving letters from Brompton Barracks [in Chatham, where Roy was posted]. By now Roy was an officer cadet and it wasn't long before he had volunteered to go to India along with David Creaton, Pam's boyfriend, and others who had been in 66 War Party in Clitheroe and were in the regular army. At this stage I didn't know Pam, but she later became a very dear friend.

Nurse Elsie Honeywell, c 1942

At the beginning of April the officer cadets moved to London prior to embarkation leave, and on the evening of April 22nd 1943 one of the office staff brought a telegram to Ward 60 for me.

It was very brief: 'On embarkation leave, come immediately.'

Sister Whitehead was off duty, but the Staff Nurse encouraged me to go to Matron and ask for leave, which I did. I didn't know if I qualified for leave after only six weeks, but somewhat apprehensively I knocked on Matron's door. Thinking about it now, Matron must have been aware of the telegram; it probably went to her office first. She was very understanding and when I asked for permission she said, "You can have as long as he has – but come back again!"

Back on the ward, Staff Nurse said, "Go and pack now!"

April 23rd that year was Good Friday and also St George's Day. I can't remember much about getting to Preston Station; I know I left the hospital before breakfast was served, so it must have been very early. I remember buying a cup of tea from the kiosk in the corner of Preston bus station before walking down Fishergate to the railway station.

Not having had time to go home first, I travelled in my nurse's blue gabardine and navy blue hat. Also waiting for the same train was a smartly dressed lady and she suggested that we travel together. Her husband was in the RAF, and she was going to spend a few days with him. I followed her on to the train, unaware that she was travelling first class until later when the guard came to inspect our tickets. The lady insisted on paying the difference in the cost of the tickets, much to my embarrassment. I wonder what happened to her, and did her husband survive the war? I think he was a member of aircrew.

We tried to make the most of the ten days of Roy's embarkation leave. We visited the two Grans and Granfer who lived next door to each other in Market Street; the aunts and uncles, Plymouth, Torquay, Newton Abbot, Wallaford Down, and we walked by the River Dart.

On the Monday, the last full day, Roy apparently borrowed £10 from his Mum and went to see Auntie Annette, to ask if she had any engagement rings in her jewellery shop in Torquay. She had only two. Like so many things in wartime, engagement rings were in short supply.

So we went on the bus again to Torquay and we came back to Buckfastleigh with an engagement ring in its little box in Roy's pocket. Not one for speeches and ceremony, he showed it to his Mum and Dad. I remember his Dad saying "Well, put it on her finger boy!"

The following day, Tuesday May 4th, we left Buckfastleigh and travelled together to Bristol Temple Meads station. From there Roy went back to London and I went to Clitheroe. I remember the train was packed with members of the forces sitting on kit bags in the corridors – no first class this time.

Back at Whittingham the next day I reported for duty on Ward 60, after first going to Matron's office to say I was back. Not being allowed to wear jewellery on duty, I put my engagement ring on a chain around my neck.

Several letters passed between Whittingham and London and almost every one could have been the last before there was a long gap. I still wrote almost every day, using the code RZHAS, not knowing if my letters would eventually arrive.

Chapter 5

One of the advantages of being in the nurses' home was the fact that the windows were only a few feet from the ground. It wasn't difficult to climb in through the window after the nurses' home had been locked for the night.

If we had planned in advance to go to the 'village hop' we could ask for a late pass, but if not we relied on clearing the window sill of anything which could fall on the hot water pipes and send the sound reverberating into every bedroom – including the Home Sister's. That would have given the game away!

We were often invited to provide some female company to an officers' mess or a sergeants' mess. Matron would pin the invitations on the notice board, and we would add our names to the list. Only a limited number could go, and Matron would give her permission – or not. We were picked up in an army vehicle and driven to the venue to join the WAAFs, ATS or WRNS who had also been invited.

There was a Fleet Air Arm base at Inskip and an Army training camp where the officers' mess was at Rawcliffe Hall. There was an interesting coincidence at Rawcliffe Hall: I recognised George Dugdale, who lived at Eastham House in Mitton, near Clitheroe. I remembered his wife Florence (née Robinson) as a pupil at CRGS (Clitheroe Royal Grammar School), and the men were celebrating the birth of their son, Stephen, a few days earlier.

That same Stephen became a good friend of our family many years later and our son John went on holiday to Cornwall with him. [Stephen celebrated his 80th birthday last year (2022)].

After experience on several different wards I found my name on one of Matron's lists. This time I was told to report to Sister Wilson in the operating theatre. There I initially learned how to sterilise all the equipment in 'Big Bertha', the autoclave.

We spent the days when there were no operations cutting and folding gauze swabs and cotton wool swabs, packing them into containers and putting them into the steriliser – no central sterilisation department as now. We also patched surgeons' rubber gloves as though we were repairing a puncture on a bicycle tyre, dusted them with talc and packed them in 'Big Bertha'. I was told to keep an eye on Bertha's pressure gauge to avoid an explosion, which I successfully managed!

'Big Bertha'

As well as Sister Wilson there was Jess, a nursing auxiliary, Nurse Cunliffe, and a Red Cross nurse, known to everyone as 'Twinks'. Twinks had a very bad limp as a result of Polio as a child. I think she was permanent theatre staff – I don't remember her ever working on a ward.

The regular surgeon was Mr Brown. He was not very tall, but short-tempered and prone to throwing instruments about. If Sister didn't hand him the instrument he wanted he would shout "Anticipate, sister, anticipate" and the wrong instrument would clatter on to the tiled floor.

During each operation we counted the used swabs to make sure nothing was left inside the patient. Instruments were also checked, scrubbed, and sterilised after each case. My first week in theatre seemed to consist mainly of haemorrhoids and cystoscopies, with appendectomies for good measure. We had to clean up after every operation.

On Saturday mornings Mr Sykes from Preston Royal came to do tonsillectomies – no antibiotics for sore throats then. Mr Sykes was a tall thin man, very relaxed, and quite different from Mr Brown. During each operation we counted the swabs as usual and also the number of tonsils.

One Saturday morning we were one tonsil short. Mr Sykes wasn't too worried and assured us it would probably turn up. That wasn't good enough for Sister Wilson, and we checked every trolley and every corner of everywhere, but no tonsil. The following Saturday the problem was solved. Mrs Sykes had found the missing tonsil in the turn-up of her husband's trousers!

When I was working in theatre Mr Brown would sometimes request blood before a major operation in case a transfusion was needed. It was my job to collect it from the Blood Bank at Preston Royal Infirmary. I was picked up by car driven by a WVS (now WRVS) volunteer. It was always the same lady I travelled with. She was from Longridge and her husband was away in the RAF. Members of the WVS were given a petrol allowance for such journeys as, like so many things, petrol was rationed.

Chapter 6

Leading up to D-Day a hospital on the south-east coast was evacuated, complete with staff, to another block within the grounds at Whittingham. The patients were mainly elderly or what were then known as 'chronics'. We assumed this left the hospital in the south-east free for casualties on the planned D-Day. They had no sooner settled in than a large bell tent appeared in the grounds, accompanied by khaki-clad men of the Pioneer Corps. Officers and NCOs then arrived, and RAMC orderlies. There were all kinds of rumours and when we were offered lessons in German, it confirmed our suspicions that we were preparing for German POWs. [Prisoners-of-War]

Nursing staff from hospitals in Bury and Oldham came to join us on the wards, and an extra Theatre Sister came from the prestigious John Radcliffe Hospital in Oxford. She was quite small in stature – but big in her opinion of herself!

On the morning of June 6th, 1944, Sister Wilson came back from Matron's office and very dramatically announced to us "It's started – the invasion has begun!"

We then worked to produce many more gauze and cotton wool swabs, surgeons' gloves, sterile water etc., and stock Big Bertha. Dressings and instruments were ready for our first patients from France.

 Troops landing on the Normandy beaches.

Several wards were reorganised, leaving Ward 60 ready for German officers, 54 and 55 for British wounded, 56 and 57 for Germans and an extra theatre was prepared for badly infected wounds.

Ward 46 was a British officers' ward. The atmosphere in the hospital as a whole felt as if we were on red alert.

We didn't have to wait long. After being on duty all day we were taken to Preston station to wait for the first batch of casualties from France.

We were grateful for the hot drinks provided by the Salvation Army. Messages were circulated: "The hospital train is on its way", then "It's just left Crewe." After being on duty all day, it seemed a very long night.

In the early hours of the morning the train finally pulled in. Some casualties were on stretchers, and some were walking wounded. All were transferred to the converted buses and delivered to the wards and the care of the night

staff. We were glad to get back to Whittingham and bed –
though not for long, as we were back on duty at 7 am.

Each German ward had one or two RAMC orderlies to
help with bed-making, dressings on various wounds and
the usual routine hard work. Ronnie Loxham, our popular
RAMC orderly, had been in the Middle East with
Montgomery's 8th Army. In conversation with one of the
POWs he discovered that 'Fritz' had been in the same
battle area – on different sides of course. Strangely
perhaps, he didn't bear a grudge!

One of the officers on Ward 60 was not a popular man,
even with his fellow officers: they told us no one liked
him. It transpired that he had been a judge in France.
Any French girl who had been caught being 'too friendly'
with a German soldier or who had helped an allied soldier
or airman was in danger of severe punishment. Our
patient on Ward 60 was involved in meting out their
punishment, and someone had shot him in the leg when
he was crossing the road. His leg was in plaster, and he
was extremely bad-tempered. Ronnie insisted that there
was always an RAMC orderly with us whenever we
attended to him.

Another officer was very sad and quiet. We understood
the reason when one of his fellow officers told us he had
lost his wife and baby during an RAF raid on Essen.

I remember one day I was sent to obtain a mid-stream
specimen of urine from a POW. Language proved to be

quite a barrier, but I thought I had managed to explain that he had to clean his private area with the Dettol before providing the specimen in the sample bottle provided. On hearing strange noises coming from the sluice I decided to go and investigate, only to discover the patient gargling with the Dettol!

Back in theatre we were very busy. Our cases mainly consisted of removing foreign bodies – bullets, pieces of metal, pieces of bone – it could be anything. British boys were allowed to have their foreign bodies wrapped in gauze and given to them as a souvenir. The prisoners of war were not given theirs, and we assembled quite a collection in the anaesthetic room.

Broken arms and legs were cleaned up and re-plastered in theatre number 2. One memorable case was a German patient who was being nursed in a side ward on his own. He had a reputation for being a violent Nazi, who threw things at any of the staff. He was obviously a very sick man – his leg was gangrenous and very smelly. He arrived in theatre number 2 and was soon anaesthetised.

Mr Brown was scrubbed up and we had student doctors from various training hospitals gaining experience and helping with our overload. It had been decided to amputate the gangrenous leg and when it dropped into the dressing bucket placed ready to receive it, I felt all eyes were on me. Mr Brown, Sister Wilson, students, Twinks and Jess looked straight at me! I quickly realized that no one else was going to pick up that bucket. And so I found myself carrying it into the anteroom and then went to look for a porter to dispose of it. The leg was very heavy – and stinking!

Penicillin was a new and exciting medicine. It had just started to be used for badly infected wounds whilst I was at Whittingham. The occasional time it was prescribed for a patient it had to be collected from the laboratory which was in another building in the grounds. It was a bright yellow liquid which had to be given by injection. We felt very privileged to be using something so new and, in those times, scarce.

Chapter 7

We listened to the news on the old radio in the nurses' home and followed the progress of the war in the newspapers. We worried about our troops in Arnhem, and especially Little Else's fiancé who was reported missing. We shared good news and bad news among the staff.

Eventually in May 1945, the war in Europe was over. I was on a German ward when we learnt of the camps at Belsen etc., and how the Jews had suffered and died in the gas chambers. The German patients stubbornly refused to believe the photographs which appeared in the newspapers and were very subdued. At the same time, they could now look forward to returning to Germany and their own families.

A typical photograph at that time

We read accounts of the celebrations in London for VE Day and there were street parties everywhere. Even Salthill Road where I lived in Clitheroe celebrated with flags and bunting, and people dressed up in all kinds of uniforms for a street party. My Mum wore Pop's (my father's name within the family) Air Raid Warden's uniform, and the group of residents were photographed by Ralph Wrigley who was a photographer for the local newspaper.

In time the German wards were emptied, and we went back to looking after British lads again. As their wounds healed they were able to go to hospitals nearer their own homes, accompanied by one of our nurses.

In August 1945, my 22nd birthday, I escorted one of our patients, a captain, from Ward 46 to a hospital in Hexham. An army ambulance came from Manchester with two FANYs (First Aid Nursing Yeomanry/Women's Transport Service) and we loaded our patient and his stretcher and headed north. I had taken my birthday cake with us, and at Shap one of the girls went into the pub and ordered four sherries to have with the cake. Our patient had been wounded in France and suffered nerve damage in his elbow. Any movement was painful, and he felt every bump in the road. The sherry and cake compensated a little bit, and he looked forward to being nearer home.

There was no Satnav and I never saw the ambulance drivers with a map, but we delivered our patient and set off for home. After Lancaster it was decided to leave the main roads and go through the Trough of Bowland. The following day was my day off and I was to be taken to Clitheroe before the ambulance returned to Manchester.

The heather was in full bloom and the girls decided to pick some to take back to Manchester.

By now it was getting dark, and the driver tried to switch on the headlights. Unfortunately nothing happened - no lights at all. The roads in the Trough in 1945 were narrow and twisting, [they still are!] not a good idea with no lights. I took turns with one of the girls to walk in front of the ambulance carrying a white pillowcase trying to guide the driver to avoid the ditches at the side of the road.

We stopped at a cottage and borrowed a torch, which helped. In Dunsop Bridge a motorcyclist saw the problem and offered to stay just in front of us and guide us into Clitheroe and Salthill Road. One of the FANYs then went with Pop to his office in Jubilee Mill to ring Manchester ambulance HQ to explain why the girls were unable to travel that night.

It was decided that the ambulance crew should stay at my parents' house overnight and drive back to Manchester in daylight the next morning. Wartime rations or not, Mum managed to feed us all. What a birthday that was!

Another time I escorted a patient by train to Romford, Essex. Knowing that the Reverend David Parton now lived in nearby Ilford, he was contacted, and he invited me to stay with him and his sister 'Auntie' Olive overnight. Olive's husband had tragically died in a motor bike accident, so she lived with David as his housekeeper along with her two sons, Bert and Ted. Sadly Bert, a rear gunner in the RAF, was later shot down and reported missing. Ted also died during the war.

David and Olive had been frequent visitors to no. 32 when he was the minister at Mount Zion. When he left Clitheroe he went to a chapel in Blackburn and we used to visit the manse in Preston New Road. Later we spent a week's holiday with them when they moved to Bakewell.

I have no recollection of how I found my way from the hospital in Romford to the manse in Ilford. I had never been to London, never experienced the Underground, but I remember the bomb damage on my way back to Euston.

I was made very welcome during my brief overnight stay. As I left, David promised he would be happy to officiate at our wedding when Roy came home, a promise he kept in 1946.

Chapter 8

For my one day off a week I often tried to have a Wednesday off.

Pam worked as a shop assistant in Redmond's grocery shop in Castle Street. David and Roy, both ex-boy soldiers in 66 War Party in Low Moor, left Clitheroe for Chatham at the same time. After Chatham they had both sailed on the SS Mataroa to complete their training for a commission in India, via South Africa. At some stage they had split up, possibly because David had developed jaundice and part of his training was delayed. Pam and I would meet in the Market Place, go to the Roebuck Café and exchange news of the boys – not that there was much news – after our coffee and chat we would go to see a film at either The Grand or the Palladium.

The old Palladium cinema – now the site of Tescos in Clitheroe

Every airmail letter or airgraph was censored, so we didn't really know what was going on in the Far East with the 14th Army. There would often be long gaps when we had no mail at all. The 14th Army became known as the Forgotten Army.

After VE Day, Doreen, Ann Cunningham and I decided to have a week's holiday in Blackpool. Ann's fiancé Harry was soon to be demobbed and Doreen's John was in India. There were still RAF boys training in Blackpool and we spent the evenings either in the Tower Ballroom or the Winter Gardens - no shortage of partners for dancing, and it gave us a good break from hospital life.

I remember during that week there was a Labour Party conference held in the Winter Gardens. One of the MPs stayed in the same boarding house somewhere near Gynn Square. I remember his name was Sorensen [later Baron Sorensen] and he seemed quite active in parliament.

Ronnie Loxham, our RAMC orderly, came to visit us on his day off. He was a good friend to us, and somewhere there is a photograph of us all taken on the North Pier.

There was a local charity run by a Preston man, Jimmy Dickenson. He would arrange for some of the artists appearing at the theatres in Preston to come on to the wards at Whittingham in the afternoons. We pushed the beds together and made a stage. We gathered as many patients as we could, the walking wounded and those in wheelchairs, to watch and meet such artists as Donald Peers, Elsie and Doris Waters (Gert and Daisy), and various comedians who gave a show and met the patients.

Jimmy Clitheroe was some relative of Doreen's family and he sent two free tickets to the Palace Theatre in Preston which we duly attended. Afterwards we went backstage and met some of the others in the show.   Another time Jimmy Dickenson organised a coach to take patients and staff to Blackpool. On the way back the coach stopped at the Halls Arms and the patients enjoyed a drink in the pub. The pub no longer exists, but I still remember how the patients enjoyed their outing when I pass where the pub used to be.

Chapter 9

Gradually people were returning home from overseas.

My cousin Jack Slater came home from Egypt and his sister Dorothy was demobbed from the WAAFs. Cousin Arnold had been in the Border Regiment and while in India had married an Anglo-Indian bride. They were now back in Clitheroe.

Dorothy Proctor from Sawley had the next bedroom to mine in the nurses' home, and just before Frank Harrop was demobbed from the RAF they were married. Several of the off-duty nurses went to watch the wedding in Clitheroe, and when they came back they told me that Mum had seen them in church and they'd had tea and cake at no. 32 before they came back to Whittingham.

Ann Cunningham's fiancé Harry was home in England after serving with the army in Italy, and they were married in Liverpool. Her room mate Staff Nurse Rose Wildman was married to her sailor and several of us went to watch the wedding in Buxton.

Letters from the Far East were becoming more and more irregular. It was only possible to guess at the reason, as letters never contained any details. But it was assumed that the 14th Army was on the move. The news on the radio was encouraging, but at the same time alarming because of the lack of reliable information.

On August 6th 1945, the atom bomb was dropped on Hiroshima and then another one three days later on Nagasaki.

Hiroshima

David Parton was on a visit to Clitheroe at the time and on my day off David and I went for a walk in Brungerley Park. I remember we talked about the devastation and the lives lost and damaged but realised it could bring the war in the Far East to an end. That didn't take long. Japan surrendered and VJ Day was celebrated on August 15th 1945.

More and more stories came to light as Japanese POWs were discovered. Many families found that men reported as 'missing, presumed dead' were in fact still alive, but suffering from diseases, sores and malnutrition. They had been very badly treated. The newspapers printed horror stories of the treatment the men had been subjected to at the hands of their Japanese captors.

Once again, we soon found ourselves on Preston station, awaiting the trains bringing us more patients. This time it was our men and boys. They were thin and emaciated, anaemic, with ulcers over their legs and suffering from sprue and malaria. Some had been involved in building the Burma railway. All needed building up again after all they had been through, but few wanted to talk about their experiences. Many of their families travelled to Whittingham to meet them again.

Our wards were full but there was a good atmosphere and no one regretted the hard work.

Not all our patients had been POWs but many had been in the 14th Army in Burma. I spent some time on Ward 46 again, the officers' ward. Captain Angus Bruton was recovering from malaria and gave me a SEAC (South-east Asia Command) newspaper when he found out that Roy was with the Bombay Sappers and Miners. He tried to assure me that Roy would soon be on his way home. How wrong he was! It would be another 12 months before Roy came home.

After Japan surrendered, Roy was sent to Medan in Sumatra. Some of the Dutch people who had been living and working in Sumatra before the war had been taken prisoner by the Japanese. Families had been split up, women and small children in one camp, men and boys in another. They had been treated very badly – as in the 'Tenko' films. One of these camps was in Medan and British and Indian troops had freed the Dutch and other nationalities and put their Japanese captors in the prison camps instead, and this was how Roy was involved.

Some of the local people apparently did not want the British Army there at that time and resented their presence, suspecting that they were preparing for the previous Dutch workers to take over again.

Each time a letter arrived from the Far East after the war ended, I hoped there would be some news of Roy's demob. Demob numbers depended on age and amount of time served in the forces. I seem to remember Roy's work number was 32. This was obviously merely a guide. When other people were returning to 'civvy street' with demob numbers much higher than 32, it was disappointing that there was no good news for Roy. Apparently, senior officers had classed Roy as 'release delayed: operationally vital.'

Then came a letter from Roy's dad with the news that Roy had been injured and was in hospital. 'Further details to follow.' It was several days later when a letter came from Roy with very brief details of what had happened and instructions, 'Don't tell Mum and Dad'.

I sent a quick letter to Buckfastleigh to tell them what Roy had written. Unknown to Roy, the War Office had been informed and automatically told his next of kin before further details were available. His injuries were not 'life threatening' but the hand grenade which caused him to be in hospital could have caused serious damage. He still bears the scar! Vital to operations or not, a replacement was found for him after all.

Chapter 10

After leaving hospital in Medan, Roy travelled to Singapore on a Dutch ship with Bob Hope (not the famous one!) Much to their annoyance, the Dutch captain told them they would have to provide their own food. So Bob and Roy acquired some army rations to keep them going until they joined the Mauretania and sailed to Liverpool.

Roy was surprised to meet David Creaton on the Mauretania after losing touch with him in India. I had a postcard from on board ship which said, 'On way home'! From Liverpool, David and Roy went to Aldershot to be demobbed and issued with 'civvies'. Clothing was still on coupons so their issue was pretty limited, a suit, a couple of shirts, shoes, a trilby and an overcoat.

Early in August 1946, I was on ward 55 with Sister Anderson. She was aware that I would soon be asking for leave and though I can't remember any details, I must have been given permission. A group of us were in the dining room at supper time when Sister O'Hara, the fearsome Night Sister, came in, telegram in hand, almost smiling.

She handed me the orange envelope. Inside was the brief message, 'arrived home, come immediately.'

Jean Openshaw, a senior nurse said she had her sister's car with probably enough petrol to get to Clitheroe and back, petrol being rationed. Jean was more than willing to give me a head start on the following day's journey to Devon. Connie Noble said she would come too, to make sure Jean found her way back. Connie was a strange, severe-looking woman; no sense of humour, a woman of mystery. The three of us arrived at no. 32 and the following morning I set off for Newton Abbot via Manchester. I can remember very little of the journey, but approaching Newton Abbot, I was determined to be first off the train. Leaving my seat, suitcase in hand, I stood in the corridor by a door ready to jump out as soon as the train stopped.

Roy likes to tell the story of how I was on the wrong side of the train, so there was no platform there and I had to wait until everyone else in the corridor had gone! I was looking for someone in officer's uniform, looking very smart. But Roy had never needed a full officer's uniform. Instead he was wearing jungle-green cotton jacket and trousers, looking pale and rather tired. The demob outfit was better!

It could have been strange being together again after 3½ years but we enjoyed visiting Gran Honeywell, Gran and Granfer Harris and the uncles and aunts again. Uncle Tom was home again from HMS Victorious where Roy had visited him when in India, but Uncle Richard was still serving in the navy.

Bill was back working with the local butcher. He had been wounded in France soon after D-Day: a sniper had seen his elbow behind a tree where he was trying to stay hidden – a pity it wasn't a bigger tree! After several operations on his arm to try to repair the damage, he had to learn to use his left hand to cut up the meat. His right arm bears the scars from elbow to wrist. [*Bill* - I remember that when he smoked, he could pick a cigarette up but couldn't let it go again – he had to take it from the fingers on his right hand with his left hand.]

Arthur was also back after his experiences with the U.S. Navy. He was working with a local builder and studied hard, passed exams and became a qualified quantity surveyor. Most of his work then meant living abroad in Nigeria, Kenya, the Middle East and Ceylon etc.

Then it was back to Whittingham for me and to start planning a wedding. The Rev. David Parton said he would keep his promise to come and officiate. Connie Noble, the mystery woman, offered me a length of white satin. No coupons required – how did Connie have connections with the black market?!

Some of our wards were now empty and closed as many staff had returned to civilian life or started training as State Registered Nurses when husbands and boyfriends were demobbed. Having served in the Civil Nursing Reserve for three years, it had been decided that nursing auxiliaries could apply for registration as State Enrolled Nurses. This meant a certificate and a pay rise. I had applied for SEN several weeks before Roy came home but it took some time before the registration came through. I seem to remember my certificate and back-pay came about the same time as I was applying for my release!

By this time, the nurses' home was empty and the remaining staff were accommodated within the hospital on the 'nurses' corridor.' Doreen had now left as John was home from India. I spent some time on nights again before being back on ward 55.

Chapter 11

Roy came back to Clitheroe and was trying to find a job. It was frustrating as to get a job he needed to belong to a union. To join a union, you first needed a job. He enrolled at Blackburn Tech and travelled every day on a crowded bus.

Mr and Mrs Greenup from 53 Salthill Road were moving to Derbyshire and asked if we wanted to buy their house. The price was £900, an offer we couldn't refuse just before the wedding. [53 was just across the road from 32.]

Wedding plans went ahead and on Wednesday November 6th 1946 Rev David Parton married us at Moor Lane Methodist Church – now the Emporium [a popular Clitheroe bar / restaurant / nightspot. I was christened there.]

The happy couple at the Moorcock Inn, 6 November 1946

L to R – Pop (Fred Broom), Amy Honeywell, Bill Honeywell, Sheila Green, Roy & Elsie Honeywell, Dorothy Slater, Annie Broom, Jack Honeywell

Dorothy Slater (cousin) and Sheila Green (friend and neighbour) were bridesmaids. Roy had to borrow David Creaton's uniform, and brother Bill was Roy's best man; the reception was at the Moorcock Inn on Waddington Fell and we went to Morecambe until Sunday. [The invoice for the reception was just under £20. Each meal cost 6/8d (33p), there were (a few) drinks for the top table, and with the taxi it came to about £19, so Pop rounded it up to £20 by leaving a tip for the waitresses. Compare that with the cost of a wedding 77 years later.]

After Morecambe it was all systems go to get no. 53 ready to move into. Wedding presents were welcome gifts to help furnish a living room and one bedroom. Furniture was only available on 'dockets' and was labelled 'utility'. It was plain but fairly good quality. We had a carpet square in the living room only and no stair carpet for several months. A radiogram on order in Blackburn did not arrive until Easter.

We moved into our own home [from no 32] in December. I went back to work for Trutex in Grindleton and Roy went to work for Moffats in Blackburn, who made electric cookers. One of the welcome perks from Moffats was a food parcel from Canada. This would contain tinned meat, tinned fruits, a packet of tea and other items not often found in our rations.

Food was still rationed and we appreciated having a friend – Pam – behind the counter in Redmans. When she offered to pack my shopping basket, I would sometimes find a bag of sugar or a small amount of butter or some dried fruit on my bill, extra to the small, rationed amount.

Travelling from Blackburn, Roy would sometimes call in at a shop on Penny Street on his way to the bus. It was a general hardware store and now and again the owner took delivery of an odd length of carpet and other floor coverings. One lucky day when Roy called there was a roll of stair carpet. The shop owner said a man had just seen it and gone home for the money to pay for it. It just so happened that on Wednesdays Roy took some money with him and so it was Roy who was able to come home on the bus with a roll of carpet under his arm. No choice of colour or pattern, but we regarded it as a luxury after bare boards for several months.

After our first few months of living at 53 Salthill Road, we gradually settled into married life. Money was scarce, neither of us earning very much. David Creaton got a job as a 'time and motion' man at Cadbury's Bournville factory in Birmingham and we were envious of his very generous wage of £8 per week. We missed Pam and David as they now lived with David's mother. They in turn were envious of us having our own home.

1947 was a very cold winter. Roy bought a warm kapok overcoat – army surplus from Iceland probably. After the Far East, ice and snow were quite a shock! No central heating of course. Our only source of heat was an old fashioned fire grate with a side oven, which I black-leaded once a week before I caught the bus to Grindleton.

The snow was so deep on some days that the buses were not running. One snowy day, Hazel Walne, who had served in the WAAFs and was braver than the rest of us, rang Mr Charnley, the head (or owner) of Clitheroe Shirtings Ltd, and told him there was no bus. His reply was "I don't care how you get to work, but if you want to keep your jobs, just get here".

So in the early stages of pregnancy I walked to Grindleton with several more girls. On arrival we were in the middle of a power cut. The warehouse and offices were cold and as the electricity was off, there were no lights either. The reps were not out seeking new orders and the local Lancashire and Yorkshire reps arrived in the offices one by one to take staff home in the middle of the afternoon. I don't think Mr Charnley gained anything from our cold walk!

I worked until summer – no maternity pay, no NHS, and no child benefit for the first child (but 5/- a week [25p] each for the second and third). I remember we had to pay for my two weeks in the maternity unit in Coplow when John was born on November 1st 1947. [Coplow was the old Clitheroe workhouse, later converted to Clitheroe Hospital and demolished only a few years ago. The site is now a housing estate.] I spent our first wedding anniversary feeling very happy and proud that we had a son.

Coplow, later Clitheroe Hospital, formerly the local Workhouse

Post-natal practice was very different then. We didn't even put a foot to the floor until six days after the birth, and I stayed in Coplow for two weeks.

Roy was still travelling to Blackburn every day and when he saw an advert for process workers at ICI Clitheroe [now Johnson Matthey, near the level crossing by the Hanson Cement works] he applied and started work there on my birthday, in August 1948. No more travelling on the bus to Blackburn, but eventually we had to get used to coping with shift work, which had its advantages and disadvantages.

In those early days we had no washing machine. Nappies were boiled in a gas boiler in the corner of the kitchen. I was lucky that Mum had her Hotpoint washer and was only across the road. We did our main wash together once a week on a Monday, whether it was a fine day or not.

I was glad we hadn't taken down the old fashioned ceiling rack and could hang nappies on the four rails to dry.

Chapter 12

Just before Pat was born in 1950, we bought a small Hoover washer. I had a small part-time job at Searson's, a similar establishment to Trutex. The machinists worked on the top floor, and on the ground floor we dispatched shirts and blouses etc., in the building, which was the National School until 1932, when Pendle Junior was built. This same building became Piccolino's restaurant (now empty). I seem to have spent quite a bit of time counting and checking clothing coupons! My small wage went towards our new washing machine.

Pat was born in Preston Royal Infirmary, and by this time the staying in bed rule was not quite so strict, and the NHS had been introduced. Once again I was a proud mum pushing our daughter to the shops in the Silver Cross pram. Bill was born in 1952. John had started school by this time, and we found no. 53 a bit too small for us. We were lucky that Uncle Will at no 55 decided to move to no. 61, and we were offered the chance to buy their three-bedroomed house on the corner – a big move, all of next door!

In January 1958 ICI offered Roy promotion to work at the big chemical factory in Billingham. We began to think of leaving Clitheroe and going to live on Teesside. We enjoyed our stay in the Northeast, found a good house in Elmwood Grove, bought our first car – a red Riley 1.5 – and made many new friends. We had good neighbours, the Zuccas and their two daughters; Mrs Morgan who encouraged me to bake my own bread once a week, and especially the Crakers at no 2. John and Ann Craker were Australian, John having moved to the UK with his work. The family are still in touch with their children Cate and Tim – indeed son Bill met up with Cate early in 2020 in Melbourne and they enjoyed a meal together. We enjoyed visiting the well-known places on the moors and on the coast, and as Roy was once again on shifts he only had one weekend off once a month, so we usually had a day out on those weekends – Saltburn and Roseberry Topping were favourites.

The children did well at Newtown Primary and I enjoyed Stockton market, especially the material bargains I found there, and put the sewing machine to good use. After being kept back a year, John started at Grangefield Grammar School and joined the Scouts, while Pat was in Brownies.

We had many visitors from Clitheroe and often entertained process workers from ICI Clitheroe who came to Billingham on a week's course etc. – Bob Singleton and Joe Joyce in particular. In 1961 Roy was offered a choice of returning to Clitheroe or going to work on Severnside. We found it hard to decide between the two offers. Severnside sounded something new; Clitheroe was somewhere familiar. What a choice! After much discussion we actually tossed a coin and in the end a return to Clitheroe won.

Once again we were house hunting. Having spent many years in Salthill Road, my thoughts were of having a change. I can't remember that we ever looked at any other houses, but one weekend Roy brought home some plans for me to look at. There had been no start on building the houses in what I remembered as Mrs Waddington's market garden, but the view of Pendle from the back of the plot convinced us that Salthill Road was still the place for us.

Pat had passed her '11-plus' in Stockton, so she started her first term at the Grammar School in Clitheroe in September 1961. CRGS for girls was a fairly new building in Chatburn Road. Roy and Pat stayed with Mum and Dad at no.32 during the week and travelled home to Stockton at weekends. By this time I was expecting Richard and so we left Stockton and lived at Peel Cottage on Eaves Hall Lane in in West Bradford until 'Wallaford' was built. We all enjoyed those few weeks together in the quiet countryside behind Eaves Hall.

Bill soon found the neighbouring Eaves House Farm and quickly made friends with the proprietors, Jim and Ellalene Aspin. He would spend hours and hours there, mucking out the cows, helping with milking and returning in July for haymaking. John left Grangefield Grammar and started at Clitheroe Royal Grammar School for boys, and Bill was back at Pendle Junior.

It was exciting getting ready for the new addition to the family. We had just a few weeks after leaving Peel Cottage to retrieve furniture and belongings and settle into our newly built Wallaford. There were many arguments ongoing between Roy and the developer, who continually tried to cut corners. Needless to say there was only one winner!

Chapter 13

After being in two different homes for a few months it was decided to have a home birth. The midwife, Nurse Wilson, kept an eye on progress, but it was her day off when Richard finally decided to make his appearance. However, Nurse Harris was contacted and Roy went to pick her up with the gas and air equipment. John, Pat and Bill went to bed and Richard James arrived one day in July, around midnight.

Pat was the first to greet her little brother and watched Nurse Harris dress him in a long white gown – no denim jeans for new-borns in 1962! I never saw Nurse Harris again; she moved to another district and Nurse Wilson retired the following week. I was sorry to lose touch with two very efficient midwives who helped to bring Richard into the world. I remember Nurse Harris said, "24 inches long, he's going to be a very tall young man!" She wasn't wrong. [He stopped growing at an imposing 6'7"]

Unfortunately, about two weeks after birth, Richard developed a problem and pyloric stenosis was diagnosed. This meant an operation at Burnley General Hospital to correct the muscle which hindered his progress - a worrying few days until he was home again. We had both given up smoking long before, but Roy restarted for a while!

John and Bill had been in Scouts and Pat in Guides, and all had enjoyed camping. Pat left Guides to give more time to school work, and in 1965 I was invited to join the Trefoil Guild. When the Guide Captain left the area, I was asked if I would consider taking over Trinity Guide Company. Nothing was further from my mind, but as our children had benefitted from Scouts and Guides, and the Guide Commissioner was very persuasive, I agreed to fill the gap. So once again (after a very long gap) I was involved in training at Waddow Hall. Eventually Low Moor Guide Company, led by Margaret Garnett, and Trinity Guides joined together for camping. To qualify for our campers' licence we first took our two companies to Ilkley where we stayed in a scout hut; then at Bowley, and in a field at Higher Hodder under canvas – all good experience. Now I am delighted when I meet my grown-up guides who greet me warmly. Trefoil Guild now goes under the name of Clover Club, still supporting guide companies and other charities.

Waddow Hall, near Clitheroe

One evening at Trinity we had arranged to hold a jumble sale instead of our usual guide meeting. Unfortunately ICI had also arranged a dinner at the Swan & Royal on the same night, so out of guide uniform and into glad rags I joined Roy and many others at the Swan & Royal. Having spent some time at Billingham I knew some of the staff from there, and found myself sitting next to Peggy, one of the wives who had lived not far from us in Stockton. When she knew I had just come from guides, she asked "Do your guides knit?" She was very involved with Save the Children (SCF), and at that time Vietnam was in the news with many refugees. She provided me with a leaflet and at the next meeting I challenged the guides to see how many little vests they could knit – or their mums and grandmas could produce – and I would give a prize. The result was that very many knitted vests were soon sent to Peggy in Stockton.

Following that I had a request from an SCF organiser in the Manchester area to start a branch in Clitheroe. 'From little acorns…' etc. In 1967 SCF Clitheroe branch was formed. I asked a few members of Trefoil to see if anyone else was interested, and some were encouraging. Four of us, all ex-Guides, formed a committee. Once again Margaret Garnett and I were working together. The regional organiser came from Manchester and got us started. We organised coffee mornings in the Mayor's Parlour, street collections, house-to-house collections, strawberry teas at Waddow Hall and the Manor House (a care home in nearby Chatburn) among others. We had support from the Council; we sent invitations to the mayors and they would turn up to be photographed, as did our MP. The local press always supported us with a write-up and BBC Radio Lancashire came to a coffee morning and broadcast live.

Chapter 14

Another appeal in which we were involved was during the time when Vietnamese families were escaping in boats and coming to England. Several families were staying in a hostel in Ilkley and SCF became involved in sheltering them and finding accommodation in various parts of England. Margaret Garnett, Dr Chris Hampson and I went to Ilkley to meet some of them as we had been contacted by SCF HQ in London. As a result of our involvement, five families were housed in council properties in the Henthorn Road area of Clitheroe.

Vietnamese 'boat people'

Churches, councillors and various organisations such as Rotary, Round Table, WI and Young Farmers all helped in preparing to receive these homeless families in Clitheroe. It was amazing how generous people were. Appeals were made in the local papers and people were donating furniture, beds and money. The first four houses were cleaned by various ladies' groups from churches, and Ladies' Circle, and volunteers freshened up the walls with paint supplied by Craven Paints in Darwen. Carpets were given, kitchen equipment arrived, and on a snowy day in January the first two families arrived.

I was still working as a receptionist at the Health Centre and quickly got to know the families, the Ngos and the Phans. Mr Ngo was a goldsmith (or did he work in a jeweller's shop?) and Mr Phan had been a cook. Dom was a teenage girl and she soon started work at Trutex as a machinist. We saw quite a lot of Dom; she would come to Wallaford on a Saturday afternoon and enjoyed learning to knit. Mrs Phan was also keen to learn to knit and surprised me when we later visited her in Leeds, as she was wearing an Aran sweater she had made herself!

Before they left Clitheroe to go to Leeds, Mr and Mrs Ngo, their uncle and the Phans invited us to a farewell meal. Howell Jones and Maxine (who were by now the Mayor and Mayoress), Roy and I and others who had been involved enjoyed their Vietnamese hospitality. They seemed happy to be joining other Vietnamese families in Leeds. We were sad that were leaving us. I often wonder where are they now? Did they return to Vietnam?

At the time of the famine crisis in Ethiopia we had organised a coffee morning in the Mayor's Parlour. Pop was in Clitheroe Hospital and early that morning there was a phone call from the Sister on Hodder Ward advising us that Pop's condition was seriously deteriorating. Torn between family and SCF, we went to see Pop and promised to return in a few hours. There had been appeals on the radio and TV for funds for Ethiopia and many organisations were holding events. We had hoped to raise about £800. That morning the Mayor's Parlour was full! People were queuing to donate money to SCF. One lady, a retired head teacher, gave the money she had saved for a holiday and in two hours the total was £1,711. Later the total reached £2,000. That was certainly a morning of mixed feelings.

Bill's note: Sadly, Pop died later that day, aged 88. Small of stature but with a big heart, he was well-respected by everyone. His former employer at Jubilee Mill, Mr Southworth, commented that he'd never known anyone who could add up a row of figures (in £, s, d) faster. A keen church-goer and member of the Methodist Church choir, he had a voice so *basso profundo* it was sometimes difficult to connect the sound with its owner.

Roy taught him to drive in the 1950s, and he progressed from a Standard-8 to a Riley Elf – a 'posh' version of the Mini. It was a manual, but Pop drove it like an automatic, sometimes setting off in 3rd and rarely changing out of 4th gear. Pat tells the story of when he'd arranged to pick her up from Burnley during her nurse training. On the way back to Clitheroe with Pat, he took the route over Nick o' Pendle, and in the thick mist as he left Sabden complained that he had no idea where he was. Continuing barely at walking pace they reached the Nick and started to go downhill, but despite this Pop was still disorientated, and by now a long queue of other cars was building up behind. Reaching the Wellsprings, to Pat's consternation, he drove into the car park. "Stop!" cried Pat, "You've left the road – you need to turn around." As Pop executed his faltering three-point turn, seven other cars that had followed him in were turning around too...!

I always thought he looked quite striking and somehow 'foreign-looking' in his youth. He was a keen footballer and treasurer of the Salthill Swifts team in the early 1900s or 1910s. The figures on the accounts make Mum's wedding reception look expensive!

Back to Elsie: Princess Anne was President of Save the Children and played an active part in raising awareness of the Fund. She came to Harrogate to preside at the SCF annual conference and to another event at the Guildhall in Preston. A group of our committee members and supporters including Miss Yorke and Miss Mundy from Waddow Hall were among the invited guests. Chris Hampson, Roy and I also represented the Clitheroe branch at the annual conference in the Albert Hall. The Albert Hall is an impressive building and we were also impressed by Princess Anne when a few of us were introduced to her in an ante-room during the interval. Roy and I were later invited to a royal garden party in the grounds of the home of the Chelsea Pensioners. H.M. the Queen, Prince Philip and of course Princess Anne were there. It was a beautiful sunny day and Prince Philip did the rounds of chatting to several groups.

Chapter 15

Mum's mother Annie (Slater) was born on 9 January 1898, the very same day that Gracie Fields was born. She was aware of this fact long before Gracie, but eventually plucked up enough courage to send her a birthday card, at the same time explaining the coincidence. To her delight the two ladies exchanged birthday cards or post cards for a few years, being described by Gracie in 1977 as 'birthday twins'. Annie's mother was herself a proper twin, born Hannah Bond. Hannah was in service at Lawkland Hall and then Coniston Hall, both over the border in Yorkshire but not too far from Clitheroe.

Annie Broom, Elsie's Mum

Annie was the perfect foil to Fred's propriety. She always had a twinkle in her eye and often an amusing piece of advice. If someone asked whether they should take an umbrella, her reply would nearly always be "If it's dry, take your umbrella. If it's raining, please yourself," and I remember once when a documentary was describing Queen Victoria and Prince Albert's nine children, she said, with a wink, "Well she must have enjoyed what he quite liked." Pop probably didn't hear or tutted quietly.

Annie died on Richard's birthday in 1995 at the Manor House, Chatburn.

Roy spent the rest of his working life at ICI Clitheroe, progressing to be Manager of North Plant and as far as I know the only person without a university degree ever to hold such a post. He spent hours poring over plans and diagrams of the works and the catalyst-making processes and knew them all backwards.

He was always considered firm but fair and could be very diplomatic at times. Process (shift) workers would clock in and out, and were paid by the hour – no work, no pay. 'Staff' were paid by the week (or month) and were entitled to sick leave. On one occasion, an employee who was also a keen angler was promoted from shiftwork to staff. Roy, his 'boss', noticed not only an increase in the number of sick days he was taking, but they seemed to coincide with whenever heavy rain had caused the river level to rise. At the next appraisal he couldn't accuse the man of taking days off to go fishing – instead he suggested that the extra responsibility of his promotion might be having an adverse effect on his health. Perhaps they should review it at the next appraisal, and if there were no improvement, move him back down to shift work. "He didn't take any more days off after rain," he said, satisfied.

In 1962 Roy joined the newly formed Clitheroe & District Motor Club (CDMC), missing out on being a founder member by just the first ever meeting. That was the start of many years' involvement in motor sport, from competing in road rallies to becoming a member of the RAC Motor Sports Association Rallies Committee and finally, on his retirement in his late 70s or early 80s, being awarded a Special Commendation by the RACMSA. He also became President of CDMC.

Early on he teamed up with the late Trevor Roberts, navigating Trevor to several victories in his Mini Cooper 'S'. Later, in the early 70's he and son Bill (who had also caught the rallying bug) teamed up in Escorts and had more success. Many good friends were made, not just in CDMC but motor clubs throughout the country. One special place was the Isle of Mull, where good friend Brian Molyneux from Blackburn started a rally in 1969 which Roy went on to compete in until the mid-1990s (when he was over 70!). The 'Tour of Mull' was described by former British Champion Navigator Ian Grindrod as 'the best rally in the world', and Mull was to become a place of annual pilgrimage for several decades.

Roy was particularly pleased in 1983 when he (reading the pace notes) and Bill, in an underpowered car on a shoestring budget, came 6th overall in a class field of well

over 100 talented crews and very competitive cars. "That's the first time the top boys have gone out of their way to speak to me!" I remember him saying afterwards.

Roy co-driving son Bill and literally flying on the Isle of Mull

Retiring from work sooner than we all expected (but he'd done the maths, of course, and realised that if he continued working he'd be no better off) he set about designing and installing central heating into 'Wallaford' and spent much of his time as the RACMSA Rally Liaison Officer for Lancashire, scrutinising routes submitted by motor clubs and using his diplomatic skills on both organisers and country-dwelling residents.

Elsie and Roy finally got around to doing some travelling too, visiting Europe with the caravan as well as North America, and for a time the caravan was very well used!

Of course Roy had fabricated wooden chocks to ensure that it was always parked perfectly level. The large garden at Wallaford was also a source of joy, but increasingly back pain too.

In November 2016 Roy and Elsie celebrated their 70th wedding anniversary, but by then, sadly, Dad was suffering from a form of dementia and living (like Annie had) at the Manor House in Chatburn. Always careful where money was concerned, he would have been horrified if he knew that he was paying for his accommodation from the results of the shrewd investments he'd made over the past thirty years. Soon after he went there he asked me on a visit "who is paying for this?" "The NHS", I lied, and fortunately he believed me. A few months later, in July 2017, he passed away in the early hours aged 94, with Elsie by his side.

After he and Gwyn had emigrated to South Africa aged 78, Arthur, the youngest brother, had died after moving back to Dawlish a few years earlier, and middle brother Bill passed away in Ivybridge, South Devon, in 2021.

Chapter 16

Eldest son John had pursued a career in journalism, starting at the Clitheroe Advertiser and Times as their 'cub' reporter in the late 1960s and rising to the dizzy heights of UK Managing Editor of Express Group Newspapers. I once visited him at his home in Hook, Hampshire, and remember him showing me the menu from the Express Group executive dining room. It almost put Northcote Manor to shame. "How often do you eat there?" I asked, "Oh, two or three times a week." "And wine?" I asked, noticing some rather nice tipples that were also available. "Sometimes I'll have a bottle with lunch." A bottle! - I said, "If I were to drink half a bottle at lunchtime I'd fall asleep at my desk!" "Not me," he replied; "Well, how do you manage to stay awake?" "Practice," came the straight-faced reply. Later I learnt that Churchill had once given the same answer to the same question, but it didn't make it any less funny.

After moving to another post as Deputy Managing Editor at Mirror Group Newspapers, John began to specialise in his favourite pastime – cruising – and writing about cruising. Gradually he formed relationships with all the major cruise lines and several smaller ones, writing pieces for various national newspapers. I was lucky enough to accompany him on several trips, including one around the Inner Hebrides in a converted fishing boat and, most memorably, a Killer Whale safari based in the Lofoten Islands, Norway. It seems strange that, after forever falling out when living at home together as boys, we got on so well once we'd left home.

One of the very many ships John sailed on.

After he retired from Mirror Group, he was asked to become editor of World of Cruising, and nowhere was his favourite motto – "Any bad day at sea is better than a good day at the office" – more appropriate. Soon after our last foray on a short cruise to the Dalmatian Coast in 2017, John suddenly and unexpectedly found himself under fire from multiple health problems and passed away a few days before his 70th birthday, less than four months after we lost Roy. He leaves his wife Sheila and two sons, Nicholas and Russell.

Pat qualified as a nurse, top of her year, then as a midwife, emigrated to Australia briefly in the 1970s and is now retired and living with husband Alan in Great Harwood. She has three children, Huw, Chris and Fiona, all married, and continued to look after Mum especially during the Covid-19 pandemic, helping with shopping and other chores.

After 'studying' biochemistry at Newcastle University – but not realising you were supposed to do any work, I failed my end of year exams and was ever-so-politely shown the door. So instead, I qualified as a Chartered Surveyor, then started my own estate agency business over 30 years ago. Married to the wonderful Valerie, we have two children, Mark and Catherine, both married and also with two children each. I've had two brushes with cancer and enough adventures and excitement to fill another book, so instead I'll move on to Richard, who after learning German and Swedish at Lampeter University (and the language that dustbin men use in Clitheroe), went on to marry Sue and become a computer programmer. Now retired, he sings in a choir like his granddad, flies model aeroplanes in his spare time and both he and Sue do a lot of walking, Richard having climbed a lot more Munros than I have (or probably ever will).

Chapter 17

In late 2021 Mum was still living at home, on her own and almost self-sufficient, but with almost daily visits from me, Valerie, and Pat. But by Christmas it was clear that she wasn't managing quite so well and, as we had a custom-made bedroom and en-suite on the ground floor, she came to stay with us... then went home again. After Christmas she came back to us, and twice went back home but each time it was clear that she wasn't able to look after herself properly.

Elsie, c 2019

The last time was when Val and I went out to Mallorca at the very end of March, but within hours of arriving there we got a message from Pat informing us that Elsie had tested positive for Covid. Fearing the worst, we quickly arranged flights back and after only 36 hours on our beloved island we were back home... to find Mum in good health and virtually recovered! But it was time for her to come back to our place for good, so she said goodbye to

Wallaford for the last time and moved in with us permanently.

Ever so gradually, old age was making its presence felt more and more. I had a cycling tour of the northern half of Ireland planned with nine others in August and decided to take a car and do substantially less mileage – but it would allow me to return home if I had to. It also meant I was able to carry everyone else's panniers, which made me very popular! The trip went well – and I didn't have to return home early.

By mid-August Mum was steadily weakening. To our surprise, to be honest, she made it to her 99th birthday on 30 August. In the evening Pat said to her "We didn't think you'd make it to 99" to which Elsie replied "Ah, fooled you then!" I think those were the last words she spoke.

Four days later, at 10.17pm on Saturday 3rd September (the second anniversary of Val's father's death and the day before my 70th birthday) with me, Val and Pat by her side, she breathed her last, and was no more.

Five days later Queen Elizabeth passed away at Balmoral, aged 96. Two remarkable lives, so well- and fully lived, one constantly in the full blaze of media publicity, the other not – but with a great deal in common, nevertheless.

Even their funerals were within two hours of each other.

We will never see their like again.

I hope you've enjoyed this biographical journey down memory lane. Elsie has to be congratulated for keeping a diary (in both senses – keeping it at the time, then keeping it until recently when she was persuaded to use the tiny writing to compile this more detailed, and interesting, true story.) Hopefully it will help to put many things into better perspective. The recent pandemic caused huge difficulties – take from Elsie's story what you will, whether it's the 'can-do' attitude, the stoicism, or the care for others, no one can doubt that she remains one impressive lady.

What I found most impressive was that nowhere in her account did she mention her rights. Responsibilities yes, but I think it's a fair assumption that neither she, nor her colleagues, at any time demanded their 'rights' in the way that many people seem to do today. We are so much better off – materially – these days, that over the space of less than a hundred years there's hardly any comparison between our standard of living then and now.

I'll leave it to the reader to judge whether or not this massive improvement has made us *feel* any better for it.

ACKNOWLEDGEMENTS

Most of this short book was written by Elsie Honeywell. The remainder and notes throughout the text have been supplied by me, Bill Honeywell. I take full responsibility for all mistakes.

Any and all profits from the sale of this book will go to one of Elsie's favourite charities, The Rosemere Cancer Foundation. Fortunately she never had cancer (after she turned 90 I used to tease her that at her age she was unlikely to get it!) The Rosemere does fantastic work for the people of Lancashire and Cumbria and deserves your support – you never know when you might need them!

Thanks also go to my siblings and our spouses – Pat and Alan, Richard and Sue, and the wonderful Valerie, for all their help and input.

Special thanks to my editor Marian Barker for helping me publish *'Elsie Honeywell's Wartime Diary'*.

Printed in Great Britain
by Amazon

37020368R00047